Dancing Naked Through The Square

Poems From the Wandering Mind of a Miller

Chuck Childers

Dedication

To the few who gave so much for so many,

SEMPER FI!

Acknowledgment

I would like to take a moment to give thanks to the people and events that made this project possible.

First to my adventurous childhood. I was blessed to grow up in a time when our favorite toy was 'outside!' A place where our imagination was unlimited, and our bicycles took us everywhere!

To the United States Marine Corps for taking a boy and teaching him to become a man. For teaching me that I can accomplish anything and giving me the discipline to do it. And for sending me to Hawaii, where I served with some of the best men I ever met and where part of my heart still remains today. You can leave Hawaii, but Hawaii never leaves you.

To everyone at the Old Mill Square! What started as just a way to get some laughs and smiles during our crazy times turned into this project. Thanks for laughing with me.

To my good friend Allen, for all those years you were pushing and encouraging me to write a book…here you go! Thanks, friend.

To all my teachers at Vinson High School in Huntington, West Virginia. I know there were times when I drove you crazy, and you probably thought you weren't getting through, but…you did! Thanks for not giving up!

To my wife, Anita. You are my anchor, my balance, and my compass. I love you.

And to my Lord and God. Whose hand I see in everything, and whom without I am nothing.

About the Author

After graduating from high school, the author enlisted in the Marine Corps. His journeys with the Marines took him from Parris Island, S.C., to Al, CA, and finally, Hawaii. His experiences in the Marines and the beauty of Hawaii have both left impressions that influence his writing.

Working at a Mill that was built in 1830 with its complex of shops and grounds has given the author another unique perspective on life. From the inner workings of the Mill itself to the effects the weather and seasons have on life around the Mill, Chuck has found a way to incorporate all this experience into his poems.

So, if you want to laugh, cry, reflect, or just let your mind wander, Chuck has something for everybody of all ages.

Table of Contents

Page Left Blank Intentionally

Dancing Naked Through the Square

Oh, at last spring is in the air. Gentle breezes blowing, through my
hair.
Living life without a care
As I dance naked through the square!

Birds are flying everywhere and sing songs we love to hear.
Butterflies floating here and there,
Dancing naked through the square!

Sunshine glitters off my face and warms me with its sweet embrace.
For some, our good time seems unfair
As we dance naked through the square!

We shake our little derrieres and act like we are unaware,
That we're not wearing underwear,
Dancing naked through the square!

It's true some people stop and stare. Some folks we even give a scare.
We act like we are unaware,
Still dancing naked through the square!

As the smell of flowers fills the air, a day like this is surely rare.
Now everybody strip, and get bare,
And we'll all dance naked through the square!

Bubble Gum Tree

After school, we run through the woods,
To a special place we love.
A magical tree we have found,
That grows lots of good-tasting stuff.

Its branches are made of candy canes,
And its nuts are bubble gum.
The leaves are made of lollipops,
That glisten in the sun.

Taffy vines hanging down,
They are always fun to chew!
Made of lots of rainbow colors,
Like orange and, red and blue!

You can have all you want,
It's always all for free.
This is a special place we love,
We call it the Bubble Gum Tree!

Magic Machine

When I was a kid, the world seemed so big,
But I got around on a two-wheeled machine.

The places I went, the adventures I had,
On my magic machine passed down from my dad.

The seat had a tear, and the bell wouldn't ring,
But sitting on her, I could do anything!

Some spokes were missing, and she had some rust,
But she got me there on her; I could trust.

My bike took me places, walking was too slow.
I would always be riding my face all aglow.

I'll never forget that magic machine,
And all the good times that it would bring!

Daddy's Little Girl

The first time I saw you such a small and precious thing.

You stole the heart right from my chest, but oh, what joy
you'd bring.

I'm amazed each passing day how fast you've grown.

Your first step, to riding bikes, you learned them all in

turn.

Holding you after a nightmare, chasing monsters from
your room.

Watched you go on your first date; did it have to be so
soon?

Now I see a woman where once a child had stood.

I would take you back in time if somehow, I could.

Daddy's little girl is what you'll always be to me.

Even though the day has come when I must set you free.

I'll always see your smiling face and hold you when you

cry.

You will always be my little girl until the day I die.

Mr. Lobster

Mr. Lobster, you are so big,

Crawling on the ocean floor.

Feeling free in the deep blue sea,

Not far from the sandy shore.

I know you're sad, but it's alright,

You shouldn't feel distraught.

No longer must you crawl about,

'Cause now you're in my pot!

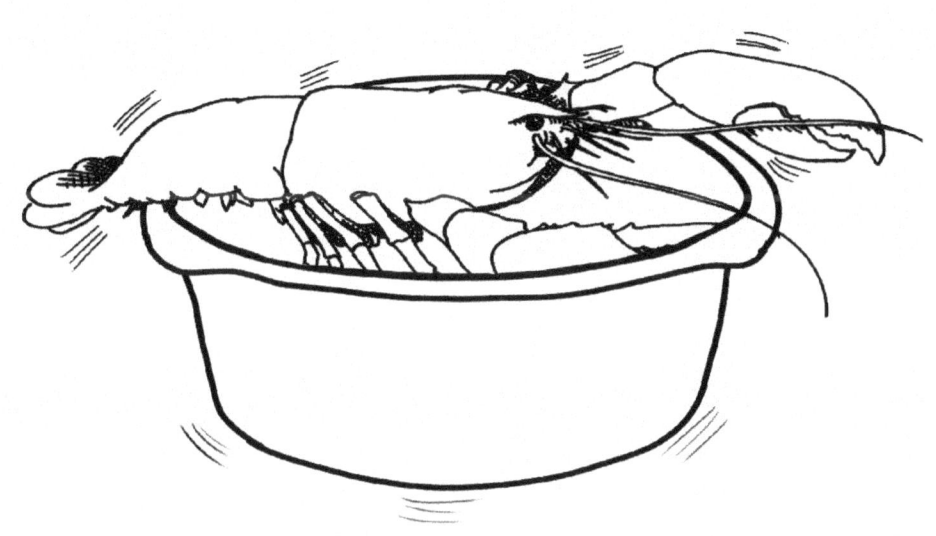

Seashore

Ocean breezes set me free

As I walk along the shore.

Feel the sun against my skin,

Makes me want some more.

Finding shells in the sand,

As my body gets a tan.

Watching all the waves roll in,

Then draw back and start again.

Children playing all around,

With laughter and waves the only sound.

Sailboats with their sails so high,

Billowing against a clear blue sky.

But now the sun is sinking low,

It sets below the sea.

And I can't help but marvel,

How the beach can set me free!

Holiday Season At The Old Mill

Twas the holiday season, and all through the Square,

Managers were busy with no time to spare.

Running around and checking their stores,

Getting everything ready for shoppers galore.

We have people cooking and baking a lot,

Trying to keep up with all that was bought.

We have got to keep moving; there's no time to stop!

Gotta stack those shelves clean to the top!

Yet through the bustle, our spirits were high,

'Cause we knew the Miller soon would stop by.

Bringing lots of cornmeal and pancakes to sell,

And while it's cooking, what a wonderful smell!

Off in the distance what's that I hear?

Is it the sound of Santa drawing near?

The sound was low but started to grow.

Then, it appeared through the fast-falling snow.

I thought it was Santa, but boy, was I wrong!

It was just the old Miller, and he was singing a song!

Off the forklift, he jumped with a bound.

He was still singing and now dancing around!

"Ho, Ho, Ho!" he shouted with a grin.

In case you didn't know it's the season again.

Bounding through the back door he made it clear,

The miller was here to spread some cheer!

Oh, goodie I thought what could possibly go wrong.

That's when he started yet another song.

He was dancing and singing like a bald jolly elf.

I couldn't help but laugh in spite of myself.

When the song had finally ended at last,

And the ringing in my ears had passed,

He unloaded my boxes and turned to say,

"I'm all finished here. I must be on my way!"

"I really must go and spread more cheer about."

Then he jumped on his forklift and gave out a shout,

"What could I do? What could I say?"

But I heard him exclaim as he drove away.

"Merry Christmas to everyone around the square.

Remember, in the spring, we will all dance bare!

Ho, Ho, Ho!"

Empty Tomb

Oh Lord I pray this special prayer,

During this amazing time of year.

I want to thank you for all that was done.

For all you went through, and the victory won!

You did it all the price was paid,

I will never forget the sacrifice made.

You paid the price that was meant for me,

Because of you from my sins I am free!

So once more I'll thank you Lord,

Because of you my souls restored.

You saved me from hells doom and gloom,

With a Blood stained cross, and an EMPTY TOMB!

Spiders!

They make their webs all over the place,

Right where you walk, so they get in your face.

You say goodnight, and I love you, dear,

But while you are sleeping, they crawl in your ear!

With eight legs and eight eyes, they crawl all about.

Whenever I see one, it makes me shout!

Some are so small they can barely be seen,

Others are the size of a vending machine!

No matter the size, when they're in the house,

The only thing that matters is getting them OUT!

I find a flamethrower can do the trick.

It gets rid of them fast; I mean really quick!

But to save your house and the place you live,

I have some other advice I can give.

Just scoop them up or shoo them along,

Outside to the garden, where they belong!

Ripples

I threw a pebble into a pond,

And watched the ripple it made.

It traveled out in perfect circles,

But shortly began to fade.

Then I threw a bigger rock,

And it made quite a stir.

Ripples traveled further,

Then became a blur.

Next, I threw a handful in

And watched them splash around.

So many ripples in the pond

Left me quite spellbound.

But the ripples got me thinking

Of our influence on each other.

The ripples that our decisions make

And how they affect our brothers!

Sunrise At the Mill

Sunrise at the Old Mill is a special time of day.
Sun rising over the mountains is quite a grand display.

Orange and yellow colors streak the morning sky.
Painting such a picture that leaves you with a sigh.

The river running gently is the only sound you hear.
These early Old Mill mornings are something to revere.

It's so peaceful in the morning, coffee cup in hand.
Time to get a-thinking and get my day all planned.

Soon, the stones start turning, and the quiet goes away.
But sunrise at the Old Mill is my favorite time of day!

Midnight Me

In the middle of the night, I awoke with a start.

Did not know what was wrong, so I looked all about.

Then, the realization washed over me,

I knew what was wrong; I needed to pee!

I stumbled to the bathroom and turned on the light,

What I saw standing there gave me a fright!

Its face was all wrinkled with bags under the eyes,

Then I realized it was me and started to cry.

Then I looked closer, and I saw a hair.

Growing out of my ear and going who knows where!

My back was all hunched, and I gave a sigh,

That's when I got a cramp in my thigh!

I turned out the light and hopped towards the bed,

Catching the edge of the door with the side of my head.

As I jumped to the mattress, I twisted my knee,

And that's when I realized… I forgot to pee!

Should I?

Do I or don't I? It's hard to tell.

It usually starts small but then starts to swell.

A feeling inside that won't go away.

For once it starts, it's here to stay.

Should I stop what I'm doing and take care of it now?

Or try to ignore it and avoid it somehow!

So, the question that's burning in my mind

Is the same question that plagues all of mankind.

The one you must answer yourself, you, see?

And the question is, should I stop and go pee?!

The Sailor

There is a broken-hearted sailor sitting at the bar.

He has been years at sea, traveling, near and far.

Now he's come home looking for the girl he held dear.

But he came back years too late, for she's no longer here.

He used to tell her stories of his travels far and wide.

She would sit and marvel, snuggled by his side.

But now he sits there lonely as I refill his glass.

He wonders about leaving, and the question never asked.

But the sea was calling; he left her with the tide.

She would have waited patiently just to be his bride.

He left my daughter standing with a silver braided chain,

On Summers Day he sailed away, and Brandy was her name.

I Like Corn

I like corn; it's a special treat.

When you pop it in a pan, it can't be beat!

Or, if you like, roast it on the grill,

Then add lots of butter; it's quite a thrill.

You can also grind it and make some meal,

Then, bake some bread that tastes so unreal.

Fry it in a pan; it's really quite quick.

Served with some chili, really does the trick!

You can can it, bake it, or make some grits.

However, you do it, it's always a hit.

In case you couldn't tell, I really like corn,

And it's been that way since the day I was born!

Ka I'I'ni' ana
(Longing for in Hawaiian)

If you have not lived in Hawaii,
Then you will not understand
About this longing deep inside.
I'll explain it if I can.

Have you ever walked the sandy shore,
On the beach at Waikiki?
Or seen the moon over Dimond Head
While sailing on the sea?

Have you seen the waves come thundering in
Down Waimea way?
Or gazed from Pali's lofty heights
At Kaneohe Bay?

From Koko Head to North Shore,
And the places in between.
Sugar cane and pineapples,
And valley lands so green.

She'll always be a part of me,
It's what I'm longing for.
The spirit of Aloha,
That rests upon her shores.

My Best Friend

He would chew up my shoes, then run and hide.

Act so innocent I'd laugh till I died.

Dig up my flowers, chase rabbits away.

I lost a good friend today.

Track mud through the house, shake water everywhere,

Sometimes, I admit he could make me swear.

And he never listened when I'd tell him to stay,

I lost a good friend today.

I lost a good friend today; I remember how he used to play.

Running around, always the clown, I lost a good friend today.

Going for a ride, his head in the wind,

Watching him, you can't help but grin.

And all he wanted to do was play,

I lost a good friend today.

He was always there when I had a bad day.

Licking my face till the tears went away.

Jump on the couch on my lap he would lay.

I lost a good friend today.

He smiled knowingly as we took our last ride.

He was old and sick but still by my side.

Licking my face one final time… and then he slipped away.

I lost a good friend today.

I lost my best friend today; I remember how he used to play,

Running around, always the clown…I lost my best friend today.

He's not around, and I feel so down…I lost my best friend today.

God's Painting

It's finally arrived, it's finally here,

And I have to say, my favorite time of year!

The blooming of spring and the dog days of Summer

Have finally made way for beautiful Autumn.

Now I can feel the nip in the air,

God's masterpiece of color everywhere!

The mountains are painted orange, yellow, and red,

Even down in the valleys, the colors are spread.

So, I'll give thanks to the Lord up above

For this wonderful painting made with such love.

And marvel at the colors dancing in the wind,

Made just for me, I can't help but grin!

Upside Down

Have you ever looked at the world upside down?

Hanging in a tree, looking all around?

Yes, the world is crazy, but I have truly found.

You can't take life so seriously when hanging upside down!

The Bunny

Hippity, hoppity, the Easter Bunny goes.

Hiding colored eggs where only he knows.

Red ones, pink ones, green ones too.

My favorite ones are colored blue.

In his basket, you will see,

Jellybeans for you and me.

And chocolate Bunnies that taste so good.

I would eat them all if I could.

But the marshmallow chicks are surely the best.

I love them more than all the rest.

White fluffy fur and big floppy ears.

He always comes by this time of year.

A smile on his face and a mischievous grin,

He comes by to hide goodies once again!

Epiphany

I had an epiphany today.

My mind still thinks that I'm 22

And can do all the things that I used to do.

Fresh out of the service, I could do anything.

With the world at my feet, I felt like a king!

But I had an epiphany today.

My body reminds me that those days are past.

The way simple things can hurt leaves me aghast.

I want to be young, run around, and play,

But my body can't do it, to my dismay.

What an epiphany today.

While my body says no, my mind says yes.

But I have to give in to my body, I guess.

It's hard to admit, even though it's true.

I have to be careful and not overdo.

I had an epiphany today!

I'm Just Me

I'm just me. I can't be you. To myself, I must be true.

No matter what this life may bring, I'll sing my song in the cold and
rain.

I may not live the way you do, but don't you worry or be blue.

Because I'm different, can't you see? I can't be you 'cause I'm just me.

Other people, all around, try to change me and bring me down.

But I have feelings. Sometimes I cry, but you never notice 'cause
they're deep inside.

I can be happy, and I can be sad, I can be sorry, and sometimes I'm
glad.

But don't try to chain me, why can't you see? I'm not like you 'cause
I'm just me.

I'm just me. I can't be you. To myself, I must be true.

No matter what this life may bring, I'll sing my song in the cold and
rain.

I may not live the way you do, but don't you worry or be blue.

Because I'm different, can't you see? I can't be you 'cause I'm just me.

The Pumpkin Patch

Pumpkins, Pumpkins everywhere,

As I walk through the patch without a care.

All these Pumpkins on the ground,

Big ones, small ones lying around.

They seem to watch me as I go by,

Sometimes it seems like they're alive.

But you need to be careful of the patch at night,

There're things in there that can give you a fright!

Be careful where you step, or you might get a scare,

'Cause I'm told, the Great Pumpkin resides in there!

Still Waving

The 1st day you flew me, you were all so proud.

You stood up to salute me and never let me touch the ground.

No matter what we went through, I'd be blowing in the breeze.

'Cause as long as I'm still waving, it means that you're still free!

Can't you see me now, still waving in the wind?

Doesn't matter what the storm is; on me, you can depend.

You may see some hard times, but I'll always see you through.

'Cause even through the wind and rain…I'm still Red, White, and Blue!

We went through some hard times; I hung low a time or two.

No matter how the storm blew, I was always true.

And I would lead you forward, from sea to shining sea.

'Cause I stand for freedom, you can always count on me.

Can't you see me now, still waving in the wind?

Doesn't matter what the storm is; on me, you can depend.

You may see some hard times, but I'll always see you through,

'Cause even through the wind and rain…I'm still Red, White, and Blue!

Rain

I like to listen to the rain,

The sound it makes calms my brain.

It's steady rhythm, falling down,

Soothes my soul, I have found.

I go and get my coffee cup,

Grab the pot and fill it up,

Then sit down and not complain,

'Cause I like to listen to the falling rain.

The Angels Cried

When God made the heavens… they were there.

On the day that he made man… they were there.

The day that Adam fell and was banished for his sin,

They were there… And the Angels cried!

On the night that Christ was born… they were there.

The day of his first miracle…they were there.

When he walked on water and calmed the raging storm

They were there… And the Angels cried!

The Angels cried in heaven teardrops fell like rain,

crying filled the heavens and couldn't be restrained.

Lightning flashed thunder roared and all were bleary eyed,

cause on that day in heaven…the Angels cried!

As Jesus prayed in the garden…they were there.

And when he was crucified…they were there.

As Christ hung on the cross and breathed in his last breath,

They were there… And the Angels cried!

When Mary came to the tomb…they were there.

And when she found it empty… they were there.

When the women saw their savior risen up,

They were there… And the Angels cried!

The Angels cried in heaven; teardrops fell like rain.

crying filled the heavens and couldn't be restrained.

Lightning flashed thunder roared and all were bleary eyed,

cause on that day in Heaven… the Angels cried!

On that day in Heaven… the Angels cried!

Round and Round

The water wheel is turning round.

Round and round, round, and round.

Sometimes, it makes my head pound,

As all day long it goes round, round, round.

The mill stones are turning round.

While turning round they make lots of sound.

Round and sound, sound and round…

All day long, going round and round.

My whole life is turning round.

Everything I see goes round and round.

Even my lunch goes round and round,

On the microwave table round and round.

Even at night, as I lay in bed,

Things go round and round inside my head!

It makes me dizzy; I have found.

All these things going round and round.

Even in my dreams, things go round and round, and round….

My Jar

I like my corn in a jar!

Corn tastes best when it comes from a jar!

You can get it from deep in the woods…. or a bar.

I can sip it while I smoke a cigar,

Or even when I'm playing my guitar!

Sometimes, I'll take it for a drive in my car.

And sip the sweet liquid that comes from a jar.

Oftentimes, I don't get very far,

'Cause sipping too much makes me feel bizarre.

Sometimes, the police will stop my car,

And ask me, "Do you know where you are?"

If I gaze at them with that look from afar,

They'll pour all the sweetness out of my jar!

So then I'll drive home and open a drawer,

And open another sweet liquid-filled jar!

Smokey Mountain Eyes

I really miss your smile and the way you used to laugh.

And those little tickle spots that made you act like you were mad.

Sometimes, you were so quiet, and you would act so shy.

But most of all, I really loved those Smokey Mountain eyes.

Then, one day, you told me one more is on the way.

Never felt this way before; what a wonderful day!

The way that made me feel inside I thought I could touch the sky.

And I loved the way you looked at me with those Smokey Mountain eyes.

The baby came and was doing fine, but you were fading fast.

The doctor said he wasn't sure how long you would last.

He said I should hurry up and say my last goodbye.

One final time, I gazed into those Smokey Mountain eyes.

As I held our baby girl, I could not stop the tears.

Knowing I would love her through all the coming years.

As I gazed upon her face, I couldn't help but cry.

'Cause she was looking back at me…with your Smokey
Mountain eyes!

Unicorns, Fairies, And Me

In my garden, the fairies play,
They dance and flutter around.
Sometimes, they play hide and seek,
And spread fairy dust all around.

While Unicorns are flying high,
With mighty wings spread wide.
The way they move is mesmerizing
'Cause they just seem to glide.

Oh, how we played together,
The adventures that we had.
Chasing Nome's around the fields,
'Cause sometimes they were bad!

From riding high above the clouds
To catching falling stars.
Our adventures took us everywhere,
We would wander near and far.

The best times were the little things,
Like sitting in a tree.
And eating fresh picked apples,
Unicorns, Fairies, and Me!

Old

I am getting older…I can tell.
My memory has started to fail.

When I walk, I hear snap, crackle, and pop.
I want to keep going, but my body cries, STOP!

When I sit down, it's hard to get up.
I just don't have the energy I had as a pup.

Lying in bed, I'll get a cramp.
Trying to stretch out, I'll knock over the lamp!

Sitting in my chair, I'll choke on my spittle.
How I manage that is really a riddle!

If you know me, just say a prayer,
'Cause I have a talent for falling UP stairs!

I have a large belly, and my knees barely work.
Causing me to walk with a shuffle and jerk.

Do not even try; I can't be consoled.
I know the truth… I'm just getting old!

Water Wheel

At the Old Mill, early in the morning, only sound is water in the
river.

Coffee brewing, ready for the day, get the stones a turning,
cornmeal's on the way.

Water wheel, turning round, oh, I love to hear the sound, water
flowing,

Down, the river keeps the wheel turning round.

All the history is talking to me, all the people working here
before me.

I can see them bagging up the meal; then they look right at me.

Man, it feels so real.

Water wheel, turning round, oh, I love to hear the sound, water
flowing,

Down, the river keeps the wheel turning round.

I see their faces sometimes in the morning, telling me about the

way they did it yesterday.

Making grits grinding corn, that old wheel is turning on, turning

on,

turning on.

Water wheel, turning round, oh, I love to hear the sound, water

flowing,

Down, the river keeps the wheel turning round.

A Day in The Life of a Miller

We wake up in the morning before the rising sun,

Because there's lots of corn to grind before the day is done.

So, we make our coffee and get ready for the day,

Then we work real hard; it's true, it's how we earn our pay.

Hear the stones a-turning; they've been grinding quite a while.

When the cornmeal comes out good, it leaves us with a smile.

Now we have to hurry up; there's no time to kill,

Sitting right in front of us, so many bags to fill!

Now the phone starts ringing, and I'll say a prayer.

Lots of orders coming in, sometimes it's so unfair.

Bag it up and send it out; it never seems to end.

As I look around the mill, so much more to send.

When the day is over and the work is done at last,

We glance around the mill, seeing all that was amassed.

In a miller's life, you can see, there's really not much glamor.

So now you've seen what it's like in a day in the life of a miller!

Christmas Magic

Where did it go?

I remember as a child a special time of year.

Seemed like everybody was filled with a magical cheer.

All the stores were decorated, the town was too,

And the trees danced with colors of gold, red and blue!

Silver bells rang on each corner of town.

I never saw anybody wearing a frown.

You could find Santa in all of the stores,

And marvel at the red and white costume he wore!

At home we would wait for the mailman to stop by,

Cause he had Christmas catalogs stacked sky high.

We would turn through the pages, seeing all the cool things,

And make a list of what we hoped Santa would bring.

Putting our tree up was always so fun,

We knew we were finished when the angel was hung.

The stockings were hung for Santa to fill.

What he put inside was always a thrill.

Then there was music, Christmas songs filled the air.

And the smell of food cooking with plenty to share.

Friends and family would gather everyone dressed in style,

While children ran around with great big smiles.

We'd lay in bed waiting to hear sleigh bells ring.

Then fall asleep dreaming what Santa would bring.

I miss all that magic, where did it go?

Can somebody tell me because I really don't know!

Millers Final Christmas

His rounds were all finished, the shelves were stocked high,

The miller sat back and gave out a sigh.

This has all been amusing, it's all been so fun.

It's still hard to believe that was his last Christmas run.

Seeing his friends and saying goodbye,

Thinking of it now brought a tear to his eye.

He thought of the good times, he remembered the bad.

And now that it was over it made him sad.

This journey is over, that may be true.

But now it's time to try something new.

Where this new road leads, he really don't know.

But down its path he knows he must go.

So, the Miller stood back, and turned out the lights.

Stepped out the door and locked it up tight.

With one last look around in the cold winter night,

He smiled and said Merry Christmas as he walked out of sight.